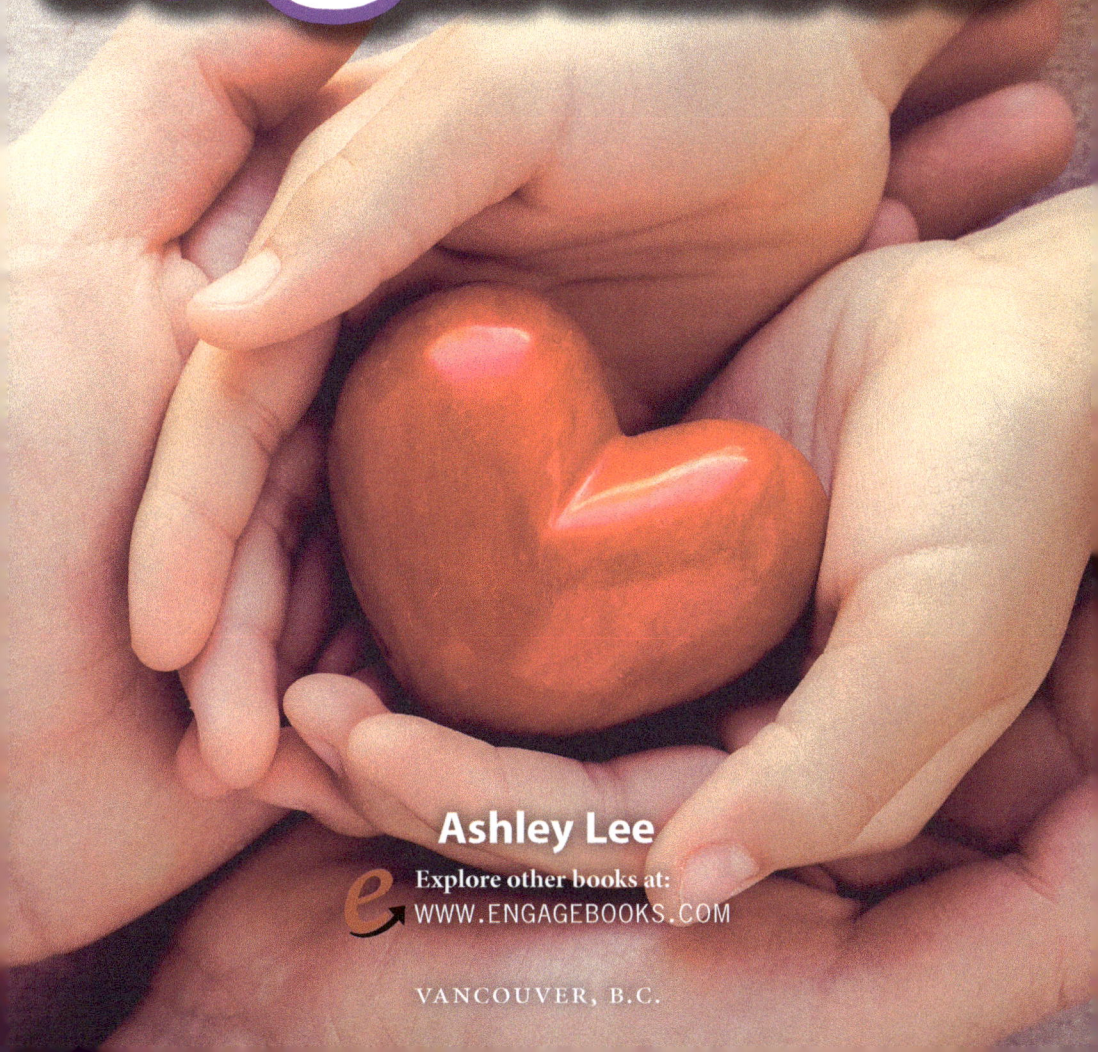

Good Character Traits

Forgiveness

Ashley Lee

Explore other books at:
WWW.ENGAGEBOOKS.COM

VANCOUVER, B.C.

e WWW.ENGAGEBOOKS.COM

Forgiveness: Good Character Traits
Lee, Ashley, 1995 –
Text © 2025 Engage Books
Design © 2025 Engage Books

Edited by: A.R. Roumanis
Design by: Mandy Christiansen

Text set in Myriad Pro Regular.
Chapter headings set in Anton.

FIRST EDITION / FIRST PRINTING

LIBRARY AND ARCHIVES CANADA CATALOGUING IN PUBLICATION

Title: Forgiveness / Ashley Lee.
Names: Lee, Ashley, author.
Description: Series statement: Good Character Traits

ISBN 978-1-77878-737-9 (hardcover)
ISBN 978-1-77878-743-0 (softcover)

This project has been made possible in part by the Government of Canada.

Canadä

Forgiveness

Contents

4 What Is Forgiveness?

6 Why Is Forgiveness Important?

8 What Does Forgiveness Look Like?

10 How Does Forgiveness Affect You?

12 How Does Forgiveness Affect Others?

14 Does Everyone Forgive Others?

16 Is It Bad if You Do Not Forgive Others?

18 Does Forgiveness Change Over Time?

20 Is It Hard to Forgive Others?

22 How Can You Learn to Be More Forgiving?

24 How Can You Help Others Be More Forgiving?

26 How to Be Forgiving Every Day

28 Forgiveness Around the World

30 Quiz

What Is Forgiveness?

Forgiveness is when you choose to stop being angry at someone. It means giving up any feelings of wanting the other person to feel bad.

Anger cannot change what happened.

Forgiving someone does not mean you forget what they did. It does not mean you think that what they did is okay.

Why Is Forgiveness Important?

Dwelling on something that happened can make you feel stuck. It might feel like your whole life is just about that one thing that happened.

Forgiving someone lets you stop dwelling on what happened. It lets you move forward with your life.

Key Word

Dwelling: thinking or talking about something a lot.

What Does Forgiveness Look Like?

Forgiving someone starts with understanding how you feel. The next step is thinking about why the other person may have done what they did.

The last step is to let go of your anger. This sounds easier than it is. But you will be able to let go of your anger if you truly forgive someone.

How Does Forgiveness Affect You?

Forgiving someone can help you feel happier. It makes you feel less **stressed** and worried.

Key Word

Stressed: when people feel uncomfortable about something that is happening.

Holding on to anger can make your heart unhealthy. Letting go of anger and forgiving someone can make your heart healthier.

How Does Forgiveness Affect Others?

People often feel bad when they hurt someone else. Forgiving someone can make them feel **relieved**.

Key Word

Relieved: no longer worried or upset.

Forgiveness can also make your friendships stronger. Forgiving others lets them know that you understand that everyone makes mistakes.

Does Everyone Forgive Others?

Some people are better at forgiving than others. Some people will hold a **grudge** for a long time.

Key Word

Grudge: a strong feeling of anger and dislike for someone who has done something wrong.

But everyone is able to forgive if they want to. It can take a lot of **practice** to learn to forgive easily.

Key Word

Practice: do something over and over again to get better at it.

Is It Bad if You Do Not Forgive Others?

Only you can choose if you should forgive someone or not. You do not have to forgive someone who has done something really bad.

But you should try to forgive others for small mistakes. Everybody makes mistakes. They are a part of life.

Remember that you may need forgiveness for your mistakes too.

Does Forgiveness Change Over Time?

Many people get better at forgiving others as they get older. They get better at knowing why someone acted the way they did.

They also learn that small mistakes do not matter that much. Their friendships are more important than small mistakes.

Is It Hard to Forgive Others?

It can be easy or hard to forgive others. It often depends on what they did wrong. Small mistakes are often easier to forgive.

Big mistakes can be harder to forgive. You often need more time to heal before forgiving someone for a big mistake.

Sometimes relationships are different after forgiveness, and that is okay.

How Can You Learn to Be More Forgiving?

Learning to forgive starts with understanding that everyone makes mistakes. Sometimes people do not mean to hurt others.

Think about how you would feel if you were the other person. It can help you understand why someone did something.

How Can You Help Others Be More Forgiving?

Forgive someone when they make a small mistake. This shows them how forgiveness works.

Tell other people about a time you forgave someone or someone forgave you. Share how it made you feel. Talk about why it was a good thing.

How to Be Forgiving Every Day

1. Try not to let small things bother you.

2. Forgive yourself for your mistakes.

Key Word

Accept: be okay with the way things are.

3. Think about how other people are feeling.

4. **Accept** people for who they are.

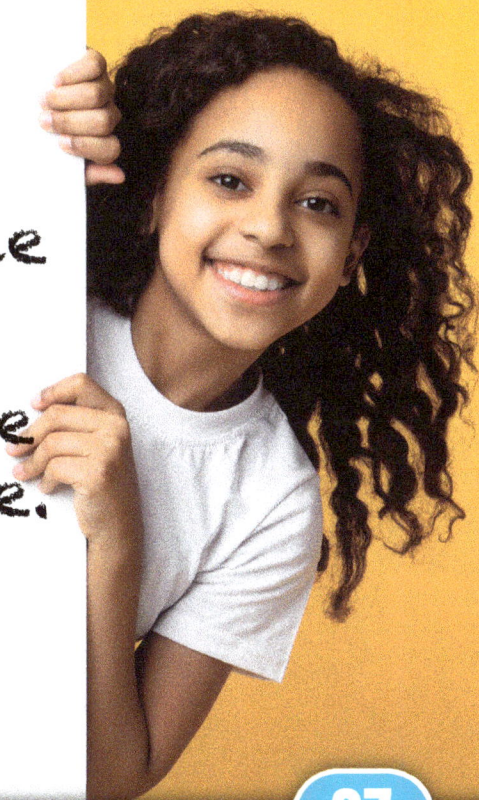

Forgiveness Around the World

People have been on Earth for a very long time. Different countries have fought a lot over these years.

Countries forgive each other for past mistakes. This helps them have better relationships with each other.

Quiz

Test your knowledge of forgiveness by answering the following questions. The questions are based on what you have read in this book. The answers are listed on the bottom of the next page.

2 Can dwelling on something that happened make you feel stuck?

1 Does forgiving someone mean you forget what they did?

3 What can holding on to anger do to your heart?

5 Do you have to forgive someone who has done something really bad?

4 Is everyone able to forgive if they want to?

6 Is it easier to forgive big mistakes or small mistakes?

Explore Other Level 2 Readers.

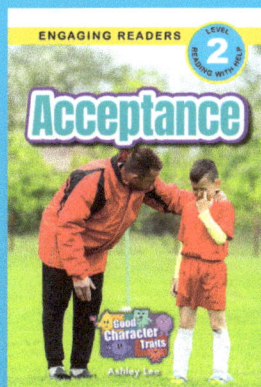

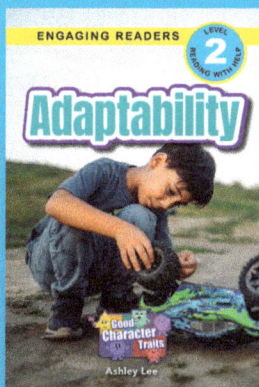

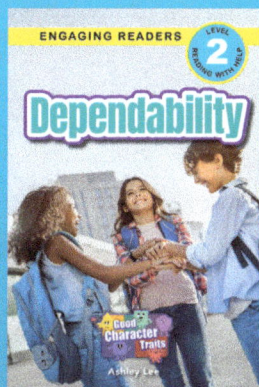

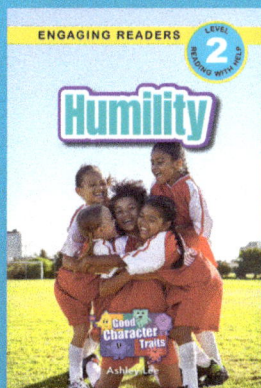

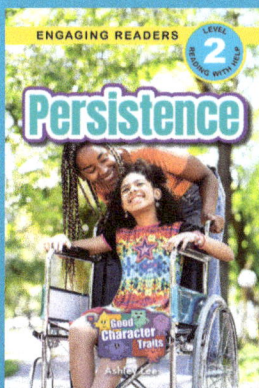

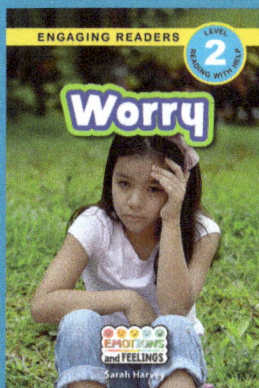

ENGAGING READERS — LEVEL 2 READING WITH HELP
Acceptance
Good Character Traits
Ashley Lee

ENGAGING READERS — LEVEL 2 READING WITH HELP
Adaptability
Good Character Traits
Ashley Lee

ENGAGING READERS — LEVEL 2 READING WITH HELP
Dependability
Good Character Traits
Ashley Lee

ENGAGING READERS — LEVEL 2 READING WITH HELP
Humility
Good Character Traits
Ashley Lee

ENGAGING READERS — LEVEL 2 READING WITH HELP
Persistence
Good Character Traits
Ashley Lee

ENGAGING READERS — LEVEL 2 READING WITH HELP
Gratitude
EMOTIONS and FEELINGS
Karl Jones

ENGAGING READERS — LEVEL 2 READING WITH HELP
Grief
EMOTIONS and FEELINGS
Sarah Harvey

ENGAGING READERS — LEVEL 2 READING WITH HELP
Love
EMOTIONS and FEELINGS
Sarah Harvey

ENGAGING READERS — LEVEL 2 READING WITH HELP
Worry
EMOTIONS and FEELINGS
Sarah Harvey

Visit www.engagebooks.com/readers

www.ingramcontent.com/pod-product-compliance
Lightning Source LLC
Chambersburg PA
CBHW052035030426

42337CB00027B/5018